The moral rights of the author have been asserted
Copyright text © Freya Haley Johnson 2019
Copyright illustrations © Tansy Creative 2019

Author: Freya Haley Johnson
(Contact: freyahaleyj@gmail.com, @freyahaley)

Illustrator: Mia Walton
Editor: Mia Walton
(Contact: mia.t.walton@gmail.com, @tansycreative)

Freya Haley Johnson
ISBN-13: 978-0-646-99784-1

CHRYSALIS

Freya Haley J

FOREWORD

This book is a small slither of the contents of my heart. This is my mind spilled onto page. In black ink, my red blood. In these words lie parts of my soul.

These words are all excerpts from my journals over the past three years. This was my coming of age, the time where I was finding my place and paving my way in a confusing world to which I never felt I belonged.

This book, this period of my life means so much more than words to me. This was a time I was in deep transformation. A chrysalis of pain and fear. After the fire, I emerged from the chrysalis into the strong woman I am today.

With love in my eyes.

From my heart to yours…

Freya x

CONTENTS

CONTENT WARNING

This book includes content that some may find triggering.
Including : suic/de, s*xual assault, r*pe, self harm, depression
and anxiety.

JUSTICE

devil

The devil danced between my lips

he opened up his shell

from his act

he showed me

how it feels in hell

He moaned into my child body

left it no longer whole

for he only feels his pleasure

devouring innocent souls

selfish

You saw her frightened eyes

chose to close yours

You felt it all

her trembling pulse

shaking lips

broken body

You chose

to put your ecstasy first

Ten minutes of your pleasure

ten years of her torment

ten years of your life

that have resisted a harrowing

plague of repercussions

For a quick fix of rapture

tearing her to shreds

it took her ten years to

find the needles and thread

to stitch up her broken body

to mend her corrupted vitality

Ten years of withered living to make

peace with the brutality

justice

My heart

fulminated

shattered

bloodied

my hollowed chest

the solemn day I was forced

to swallow a harrowing truth

Justice will never exist to me

others will experience my same pain

Justice may not exist for them

A frightened child saw that concept

fade away in spiralling smoke

the shadow of the man

who locked the bathroom door

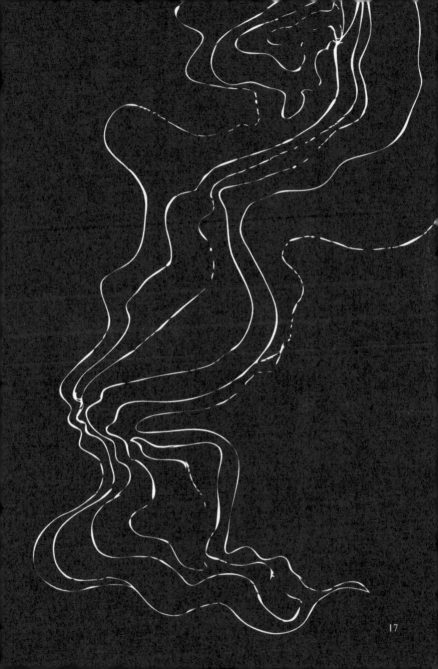

the devil down the hall

He still inhabits

the room down the hall

I hear floorboards creak

when the night falls

Drawing bumps on my spine

electric my fear

my pulse, she falters

when I sense he is near

Picking the safety locks

he tears down the walls

underneath my covers

I'm crooked and balled

I'm hiding in terror

taken by bliss

echoing in full rooms

lucifer lends a kiss

Walking the earth

on footpaths of nails

it's agony to live when

only persecution may prevail

He possessed me, brother

being done with you

devoured my innocent mind

finished in me too

Your shrill screams of heaven

heart loomed by pain

settle heavy in this house

where I'm forced to feel you again

intimacy

Every man's touch feels like

that beast

evil whom possessed you

Loving embrace means so little

whilst envisioning his capability

of the same depravity

His rose petal touch

would turn to iron prongs

as I feebly mutter "no"

So I push it down further

force myself to feel fulfilment

Sometimes I feel like screaming

yelling

Every stroke is a scalpel

dissecting further

digging

searching for what little

you may have left me

ink

Sharpened nails: brushes

Tender skin: a cotton canvas

I can't help but enjoy the feeling

find freedom

in opening myself up

making valleys of crimson rivers

a white dove

stained red

by ink of ignominious quills

hourglass

Death compasses

painted in loaded arrows

south in magnetic attraction

to mortality of a widowed kind

I've lost my love

I've lost myself

It feels like each day my soul lies

with hades tangled in passion

on his bed of skulls, I lie

I'm trying to remain unafraid

unscathed

it just feels as though my time

my hourglass

is running dry

my darling

Whispers of places where I would feel

safe

happy

home

"The knife by the counter

the bathtub, darling

the great ocean waters are

perfect for drowning!

The pills in their tubes

the cars, my darling

down dawns highway

the trains, they are passing

the buildings they're growing

taller; I'm starving

would it be a chore

to fall for me, darling?"

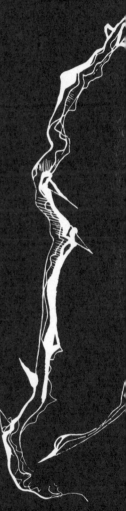

nightmare

Last night I slept

on a bed of thorns

my eyes clamped shut

in vivid reality

his claws burying

themselves in my muscle

water down my cheeks

the silent echoing screams

an oblivious child

failed to muster

his eyes were ravaging me

his dead soul

hungry for the light in mine

I felt it all

In my dreams

he still tortures me

return

When he returns my head will

hold high, eyes dry

wrinkling only in smile

touched only by my tender talons

or those of whom I love

It feels as though

all the strength I grew

all my fortresses and defences

were sandcastles build on eggshells

Crumbling when his callous shoes

stomped through Persephone's gates

Border Security

The knives in his eyes

remained undetected through arches

through conveyor belts

the whole force couldn't

protect me

My safety is under threat

from an overseas terror

returning home to pillage me of it

finally

The knives in his eyes remained

undetected

by everyone I knew

I worry that only my eyes

may see them

drink me

My words are my weapon

black ink: subtle poison

It's a slow riving death

You'll read my words

they'll linger in the confines of

your mind

the same fashion in which

your shadow paid rent on my left shoulder

Each letter a guilty brick

I place on your feeble shoulders

which poem, I wonder

which word

will eventually break the spineless man's back

comfort

I found comfort living with him

the peace in being a victim

stormy ocean rain

feels safe

when you're used to

a hurricane

coals

I grew up

with coals in my throat

igniting my voice box

as I let

air escape

Living as mute

under anvils of trauma

carcass

The trumpets blared

ancient war cries of death

for ants and flies

they travelled

to pick apart my flesh

Viking horns blowing

on these cold, limp bones

decomposing, devouring

the vessel I once called home

black owl

I am shiva dancing

in the darkness

waiting

watching

grey smog

fatal mist

One day I return

with skulls on my hips

to wreak havoc on those

who harmed me

I am the black owl

swooping him in clawed talons

my curved beak

will spoon eyes from their sockets

rip into their flesh

the way they ate my vitality

I am shiva dancing

on a pointed compass

in the next direction

I will dance on their graves

and finally get my justice

PHOENIX

grace

Every day since trying to leave

my earthly existence

I've found my head in the heavens

my arms outstretched

singing

"GRACE!"

"what a beautiful day to be alive"

phoenix

Inferno ravaged my land

only ash endured

grey and desolate was my

life and mind

until I awoke from your slumber

in purple fog, a miracle

I rose like the sun

over the misty mountainous horizon

A crimson phoenix

reborn stronger

from the hellfire

I expected would ruin me

cherry

My body has never been

a tool of exploitation

a red cherry to seep your fangs into

juice drips down the length of your lonely thigh

though that has never been the reason why

I feel the air meet my pores

all of them open with love

My body has never been

a vicious dagger

a dangerous creature

a weapon of offensive destruction

avert your eyes

women are evil in disguise

apparently

See my body was ripped from my cradling arms

at a tender year

along with it my security, my trust

a life lived long in fear

Just when I rose

with a new lock and key

a new door for my love

to inhabit this body

I've been spat at

called

slut,

whore

and more

for living in the skin

the scales I was born in

My body has always

been my home

not an instrument for you to

vandalise and demean

let me be free

let me be me

it is not a crime

My body is a rental

for my soul whilst I'm alive

and I'll be god damned

if anyone ever tries to evict me again.

paralysis

I'm no longer afraid to sleep on my back

for no demons will sit on my chest

no creature will claw at my breast

and devour my lungs raw

home

the word home was stolen from my vocabulary at age seven

I'm finally learning the meaning

my new home is

a two bedroom in mossy green

it smells like the last meal we cooked

the fridge always feels a little too empty

where we grow into

liberation

creativity and

peace

reminders of a harrowing kind no longer plague me in this

sunny spot

I can dance

paint and

sing as I please

sleep without worry of footsteps and creaking floorboards

here I am safe, here I am home

I can't express the relief

path

I have trodden

in muddy puddles of stardust

along the divine path

back to myself

I have ached and

deformed myself

along the divine path

back to myself

I have danced under

the light of strawberry moons

releasing pained howls

of childbirth

Whilst finding

myself

already wombed within me

burning

Nudity empowers me

I feel myself burning brightly through my exposed skin

I feel human

connected

A point of vulnerability I conquered

I accepted and moulded

into empowerment

I once looked at my body in disgust and shame

in my budding breasts

I saw his lingering eyes

in my mouth

I felt that shame

in this flesh filled moment

I am the only creature

that lives on in this skin

What a glorious feeling that is!

I won't keep quiet

(for N)

If I make you uncomfortable

with my story of pain

know that my words

may never be restrained

No, I won't keep quiet

when there's work to be done

too many people are hurting

in catching webs he spun

So I tell all my story

open your ears

learn from me how it hurts

feel the weight of our tears

Everyone I know

has a story like mine

it breaks my beating heart that

there'll only be more in time

No, I won't shut up

'till I sleep in my grave

not until rapists

learn how the fuck to behave

No one can understand

the hurt that ensues

the torment and torture

after being abused

No, I won't keep quiet

I won't be polite

when so many are hurting

it's my duty to fight

Against those demons

who consider it just

who think it their right

to break their lover's trust

Against those demons

who say they were drunk

"I don't really remember" they say

"its not my fault"

Against those demons

who lurk in the streets

looking for some scared person

to conquer

fuck

and beat

Against those fucking demons

in positions of power

who are older, wiser, who should know better

than forcing us to cry and cower

No, I can't keep quiet

and I certainly can't be polite

when rapists walk freely and

survivors remain in plight

Until we are free

until everyone knows it wrong

my voice will be here

here, loud and strong

proud

be proud of yourself

you have made it this far

your strength is intergalactic

admire yourself

you deserve infinite unconditional love

surrender

I sank my weight

deeper and deeper

under imaginary waves

lapping at my thighs

flooding my lungs

How did I believe

such fallacious fiends

formed as matter and air

could consume me?

I resisted the evil that

dwelled in myself

the shadow

skeletons

cracking their arthritic bones

in the warm up to emerge

from closed cupboard doors

I should have surrendered earlier

for fighting drains you

of your heroine blood

dripping

drop

pools from your slit throat

by the knife of resistance

of creative mind

sizzling as they hit warm earth

sometimes surrender is necessary

when what you resist plagues your mind

experience that pain you fear

grow past it

for bones and blood

make a great fertiliser

surrender but never give in

for giving in is weaknes

where waving the white flag

is strength

firefly

A pained and painted crimson past

the lowest wavelength resurfaces

echoing over glass rim

whistling through cracked

windblown lips

the tired eyes of a caged tiger

drugged and senseless

It's still there

compassion like a ship of frightened cattle

leapt over fences into your

hopeless dusty eyes

dried tears of a nation

my heart shrivelled under desert sun

roadkill over dotted lines

Under Wheels

Under Wheels

I'm Under Wheels

my furry decapitated limbs

The only hope for a gracious heart:

a loner firefly

amongst low lying shrub to whom we tether

safe in our ribcage

to light before brown eyes

When it's time to feel

the weight of the world's darkness on your shoulders

the pain of duality in your chest

Let the fireflies feast

for peace grows like a rabbits den

This fly I hold between two lungs

is a match in grey smog

so that I may forever remain

A four-leafed clover

in a dried field of three

bridges

Along this path of yours

haul yourself over my ribs

arched in afternoon sun

you'll find

the grass greener

over my bridged back

you may walk

over saltwater crocodiles

ancient dwelling

at the base of my spine

but I have hiked this route before

this trek of death

fear and the mind

so find comfort in knowing that

Along this frightful journey

my gentle heart did survive

naked land

I am not the wheatgrass

frail and dry and meek

to ash

she turns

when fire burns

but I am not so weak

Among the sweet eucalypts

a cumbersome leafy grandmother tree

standing tall

she does not fall

her strength makes home in me

I am the weary traveller

blistered under southern sun

my skin may be peeling

though I can't help but feeling

my journey has just begun

I was the red dirt land

plains plundered by cities

though now I know

I too can grow

I will rise in adversity

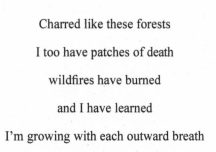

Like the barked bodies

rooted and sun-kissed

my fingertips high

grasping the sky

grateful that I exist

Charred like these forests

I too have patches of death

wildfires have burned

and I have learned

I'm growing with each outward breath

FORGIVENESS

sympathy for the devil

I'm Learning to forgive. Learning.

I'm proud I have acknowledged that I still hold on to past pain

I'm grasping at any rope that anchors me to my deepest
trauma

It's forcing me into stagnation when I should catch the wind
and sail further

The most influential happening of my life is simultaneously
the most painful

My past is painted in red ochre silhouettes of a childhood
devastated by insecurity

By the construction of trust to be built around boys who hurt
me

When we hate others

we give them power

power over our love

power over our anxiety

our sleep

our minds

We give them the power to rule our motivations

hatred allows them to form in the shadows we cast

following us as a

cloud of masked insecurity on

every step we take

So I'm learning the tricky art of forgiveness

I'm learning to release my heart from the traps of blame and

hatred

to those who have wronged me

I forgive you

Because I have come to realise

they must be in more pain than I, to inflict such suffering on

others

I once lusted after blood

though I no longer wish for revenge

I wish that they no longer be plagued

with the disease that forced them to corrupt me

I know the cards of justice will be drawn

perhaps in a different life

perhaps in some subtle way to which I will never bear witness

I accept and trust in this

So I will not hold on to it

I will let go

The pain they caused me remains wombed in the past

I decide in my present

their inactivity in ruling my actions

I will not sit idly by to allow my life to be lead

through the eyes of hatred

For that is not my purpose

I've been saying this for years

I will not let them own me

in possessive ignorance

hatred fuelled my bones and

pumped my blood hot with the promise of violent revenge

Now is the time for a new leaf

I, the great tree, bloom and grow with love

To my abusers:

I forgive you.

I send you nothing but the hope that you will heal

that your illness will surrender to love

so you and others will recover

just as I have

bambi

He tells me I'm weak

whispers through his forked tongue

about how I struggled to get up

when he threw me

across the room

spit and tears making home

on cold orange tile

How pitiful it was to witness

bambi beside the empty bathtub

kneeling as if in prayer

yet my knees felt cold in confusion

What were they doing?

just being boys, I suppose

being mean to me

boys will be boys

and I shouldn't take it so personally

they know what to do with me

He scoffs

I'm pathetic, he thinks

to have let them all take advantage of me

I'm pathetic and weak

to have remained kneeling

through blindness and gag reflexes

I'm pathetic

with white sticky stuff

fouling my tastebuds

yes, he thinks I'm pathetic

for I had no reason to believe that

I was anything more

He's choking!

with laughter, lord it's hilarious

"she sucked his willy like a lollipop!"

whooping, the children gasp for air

And I'm sitting motionless

mortified

he was meant to protect me

I wonder, is it some form of self preservation

which calls for you to harm me?

some whisper of immortal security which promises itself

in the valleys of emotional projection

God, he tells me I'm weak

though I wonder if he would persevere like I have

through mere half of what he inflicts

on the weakling bambi

he deems bloodied and broken

ice skating

Below the frosted white lake

in crisp winter he resides

biding his time

biting his claws

Some days you walk over ice

admiring the birds

their beauty

reflections of the clouds in

glistening glazed mirrors

Through tinted vision, he will

gaze upon your beauty

envy the way you

spin and stride like you're

skating

over the very surface that holds him prisoner

Sometimes he may boil over

with such rage

his heat forms cracks

under your feet and

forces you to feel his depths

Splashing and cold

you gasp for air

through spluttering blood

which he tastes metallic

sharp over his tongue

like guilt

regret

self-loathing

fear

He loosens his grip

lifts you back to chilled air

retreating

melancholy

to watch you glide some more

and admire your perseverance

Until the next cloudy day comes and

he misses your light

he wants your warm delight

in the dark dreary waters

buried under the surface

chamomile

The parts of you that are hardest to love

are the ones who need it the most

The people who are the hardest to love

are the ones who need love the most

compassion

When you learn what it is to love

fully

openly

truly

you understand reasons behind all actions

the motivations that form hostility

you learn to feel compassion

empathy

Its all ruled by fear

reactions not actions

you can no longer blame

but pity

their wrong doings

for you know that they

only suffer from

a lack of love

untitled healing

My insecure shadow self resided

deep in the caverns of my heart

every small pang of rejection

jealousy or insecurity

was buried

she felt the pain piling her stomach

she grew too cumbersome for that cave

forming cracks in my limestone fortress

The day my walls fell

I fell too

Blinded by the capacity of just how horrible I could feel

in denial, I deprived my shadow side of love

now I must learn to nurture her

to love all aspects of my being

seeds

I feel clover seeds

growing daisies in my pores

the arctic winter

and ice has melted

surrounding my heart

she's beating warmer now

my spring is here

weeding

Some words for those

who believe it wise

to criticise

what they see in my eyes or

the slither between my thighs

who know it their place

to spit my name in disgrace

like they've met me before

had a quick taste

of my ether

my mind

they know nothing of my kind

But they chat

babble

blubber and

boil over

with juicy concoctions

of falsehood and drama

in cauldrons of herb

cultivated in greenhouses

where hot damp air

is thick with insecurity

inside this glass box

Why do you care

to deflect insecurity on me

when I am growing

over the barbed fences

on my terms

in my field

which I tend to

with a green thumb

an open heart

Could it be the dissatisfaction

inside your belittled garden walls

that makes you want to tear

my petals down

watch my trees fall

so you may bury them

six feet under the dried up

soils

In your mind

I'm more useful below you

Instead of notions

judgements placed on my sunflower garden

perhaps its time for some renovations

weeding

inside the borders of your own

castles

Stain glass windows

draped velvet crimson

hanging fabric pulled tight

to block the worlds darkness

with it the worlds light

whispers of hope

slither through

illuminating

the dust swirling through stale air

The ghost of a prince strides through

echoed rooms of gold and turquoise

surrender comes first

Your head bleeding on a spike

crucifix melting in black tar

with it your sense of hope

your world crumbles

castles falling to fear

It feels too much like before

you wonder if all this labour

was built for ruin

the hired builders

brick on brick

the embellishment

reduced to shambles

beneath your earthly eyes

You clumsily drown in your motes formed of tears

waters of emotional damnation

every insecurity

every pressured smile

every cell of ignorance

is empty in this room

where thrones are burned

surrender is pure

in the bloodshed amongst shit stained corpses

surrender is peace for both sides

of psychic wars

999

Whatever you fear

you eventually attract

These steel ropes I knotted to Pandora's box

fell further and further

down the well behind my mind

deeper in heavy waters

I struggled to hold on

drawing beads of sweat

Bloodied

blistered

splintered

peach hands with dark empty patches

through caging fear

boxing insecurity

gripping so tight

when letting go would inflict less pain

I release fear

I trust the divine path laid for me

I would walk blindfolded

on a tightrope over scorpions

if it allowed me to evolve and heal

shadows

After shadows

cast in afternoon sun

we experience the night

our shadows dissolve

into tangible reality

Our fears surface

our insecurities

our roots

buried in clay soil bodies

awaken and live again

rise from

neglected tombstones

To search for the love

the peace

the healing

they were deprived of

Deprived as we buried them

before listening

before learning

they needed love to be released

Night brings everything to light

in the night

we honour our plight

we do not fight

They are a part of us

We accept the darkness before dawn

then sun rises again

submarine

I am healing

finally, truly healing

formed by the cosmos

a composition of compassion

I no longer hold onto safety within paranoia and fear

there was far more to uncover within

oceanic abyss

than fathomable with a terrestrial mind

I am the submarine who braved the blackness

dark murky waters of self-hatred and terror

Travelling in this vessel of light

I see creatures of below

beauty within my depths

discovered growth and life in blackened places

I thought impossible to be fertile

Amongst them: a golden thread of seagrass

formed by cotton as courage

I stitched up my wounds

closed my skin

under alien blue

my gashes turned to cuts

my cuts healed to scars

my scars became patterned skin

a sculpture of strength and tenacity

I journeyed to the caves where my pain was rooted

weeds crowding my gated Eden

so I wore my best gardening gloves

and ripped the roots from my chest

open pores to rest new seeds

A beautiful garden is sowed there now

LUNA

16.1.16

Lights ripple across moonlit water

feet dropped off the roof

childlike giggling

lips on lips

you

I felt

reunited

collided like my atoms

had felt the touch of yours before

No, I'll never forget how that first one felt

fingertips

Beautiful

when your fingertips feather

the outlines of my body

making circles

invisible art

on my tainted canvas

He has allowed me to realise

finally I am able to be loved

wholly and truly

red

It's raining ash now

a fire burns somewhere

the smokey sky

turned the sun fire red and

in his vivid light

I saw my own fleshy heart

beating bright red

filled to the brim with love

sacrifice

Under the shelter of your

winged arms

I fumbled the words

through glassy vision

broken phrases stuttered

through dampened lips

the times I've been hurt

detailed

despite my shaking core

trembling hands

beaded sweat

and streaming eyes

I tell you

I feel safe here

It rings truth

on singing bowls

which contents include:

My bleeding heart

amethyst

and sage

a sacrifice

left under the moon

for howling wolves to send

my world to you

oceans i

Under moonlight, I moved

illusions of self-motions

molecules of my water

marrying with these oceans

as I slept

a dreamy midnight swim

the currents pulling my body

mermaids singing his hymn

on the shores of venus

my waves crashed blue

glistening turquoise water

my tide towards you

oceans ii

His mop of curled hair

throbbing underneath the surface

catching rays of light

in poseidon's eyes under neptune sky

We swam together

kicking up sand with our tails

dust floating towards the sun

where we follow to catch our breath

and a few sunlight kisses

on our skin

waves form in his eyes

so deep they hypnotise me

starving

I was a starving child

hungry for fulfilment of a loving variety

ravenous for safety of an unknown persuasion

found in a deep solace with you

through my infatuation

I learned to spoon feed my silenced mouth

nourish that abandoned child

with self love

acceptance

and all the magic I needed

to open my heart

journey

The train smells like

a lifetime ago

of hard long days

carrying cappuccinos

Soft warm nights

in arms of love

like anticipation

for some unknown location

the need to sit in silence

We disconnect from the journey

it smells like the only

smoker in the carriage

we find it hard to bear the journey

when home is all that keeps you on

the 910 past 6

the freo line in peak hour

Phones and headphones

books and bags

some faint whiff of piss

Though it does remind me

of a certain stranger

familiar candle lit

in the black pupils

of old age

He smiles at me

as I observe the people in suits

make up stories for their

mundane routines

He smiles at me and

perhaps asks

how my day has been

chats about his children

I, the humble train dweller

have open ears for this sort of thing

for I can tell

from his smile

I am not the only person

who enjoys the journey

lava

A great sigh from your chest

a sob erupts from mine

bodies of magma

boiling up my bones

for ten years

releasing and spilling lava

the day she turns active

solidifying rocks on your chest

I glimpsed a gentle tear

in the corner of your eye

you didn't know I could

but I think you cried

not because you pitied me

but because you understood

to my sick friend

Even with this disease

eating up parts of your body

you are whole

chewing on your perseverance

just when you feel like you've lost motivation

it spits you out again

you are never a burden

I will be there

in waiting rooms

sterile hospital beds

Wherever you say you need me

I will unconditionally support you

in ultrasounds and endoscopies

I will be there

rain

I didn't know I missed morning rain

until it fell on Monday

clean, forest smell

gentle hum of water falling on earth

fills my heart with a sense of nostalgia

reminds me of that gentle Sunday

when it was impossible to crawl out of your arms

and droplets collected on your window

heavy

I'm heavy when you're high

paranoid when I breathe you in

I'm shaking, icy, fucking paper thin

I know I should be happy here

held in your comforting grasp

I found love inside a metal dome

until heated plastic burned my heart

God, they hurt you too

but you couldn't see

blinded by another tab

long lost

not to love, not to jealousy

No, I lost that boy to the weight of

worry on my shoulders

He became lost in a tunnel

a cylinder of destruction

the sort that buries your sanity

buries your reason under

soil of escapism

So I'm heavy when you're rolling

pained when you're patrolling

the cage inside your head

you're in too deep to even see

these drugs, my love

they're hurting me

I miss the light in your eyes

your goofy smile

which never fails to widen mine

I love you, I do

but I can't love a shell

a skeleton

I catch glimpses of you

the next time you're fucked up

God it pains me

to only see you when

you're so far from your sober self

I love you, I do

But I can't love a skeleton

While I'm alive

I'm heavy when you're high

under cancer sun

I'm at sea

without compass without crow

I yearn for softer waters

for gentle breezes

for summer skies

light and

his sunshine warmth

an evening in me

embracing my water

the cold, fearful depths of my

Pisces moon

to me, he'll whisper

that I'm safe here

In those arms

I worry not of the storms

of lightning and when

the power is put out

but of

the candles I light

in blackout

the glistening

reflected on

calm clear ocean

Cradled here I mostly

think of his heartbeat

and how beautiful it is

to feel that on my breast

luna

The gentle moon

was a stranger to you

before you saw

the way she spoke through

my lungs

The liquid white

kissing my highlights

pink and pale

She was a stranger before

you saw

her phases shifting

like my temperament

My new moon softness

fragile eyes

shifting in shadows

My full moon fierceness

making shapes

at midnight by the ocean

How I pulled the tide to crash at your toes

Yes, La luna was a stranger to you

before you fell in love

with

her light in me

before I untied your

blindfold

and whispered

"doesn't she look beautiful tonight"

moby dick

The first time I left you

it was fear

of ropes that promised

entanglement

at such a tender year

it was fear

fear of what I hadn't faced

during the beautiful distraction

that was you

it was rash and sharp

like the first time

I pierced my velvet skin

with rusty scissors

The second time I was with you

it was the high socks I used

to cover my bloody ankles

I was poisoned water

cracking slits in wrists

with soiled fingernails

scratching

the walls of the dam

The second time I left you

it was real

it was the whispering promise

freedom of an open legged kind

it didn't take long to learn

letting people in

I felt weaker

pathetic

bruised and broken

scarred and bloodless

the subtle discovery of ravens in my soul

So I called you a third time

with my ivory conch

to beg you

please

don't let me face this alone

The third time I loved you

I died in your arms

it was hard to love

a mortal man

I was in a labyrinth

the maze of my mind

the candle I held before my eyes

was you

Then came the third time

I was forced to leave you

air escaped through quivering lips

as I told my light to leave

O the darkness swallowed me whole

like a whale did

Jonah

the belly was

lying on cold carpet floor

The third time I left you

my love, I left myself

until I was forced to see

the candle I held

was within me

stew

I knew

the moment it started

that it would end

nothing would prepare me

for the way it slithered through my arteries

tore out my heart

I ate my insides

cooked up my words

when I made that decision

Change is hard

we grow comfortable

until we stop growing

we need new soil

a new place to sprout from

as much as my old place

may have felt like home

filled my heart with love

I need the new to make sure

I grew this happiness

from my palm

it isn't

stemmed from you

Though I regret nothing because

the security

I placed within you

needed to be rooted

in my fertile soils

not yours

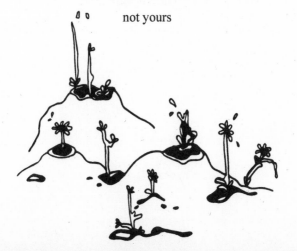

candle

You need to redirect your heart

send love to yourself

you are deserving

of your glowing soul

you are deserving

of your unconditional love

I have learned that

until we find self-love

we cant love others

without hurting ourselves

drums

Beating to a different pace

alien longing

in chambers of muscle

aching from a new regime

it may take time to adjust

to the new rhythm

but

it will make

your soul dance

maybe even more than before

nectar

I, the gentle moon

once drank the light

of a lover

To feel brighter

in weathered scales

sipped at his

solar nectar

I learned to be full

after three months

of new moons

O to find glorious sun

had been in my heart

beating this whole time

push

I'm used to ulterior motives

they want

my face

my curves

my healing

my status

Eating up my flesh

licking my rotten bones with poisoned tongues

boiling my leftovers for stew

Indeed, you were right

I did take you for granted

I only saw my projected illusions

opaque over your pure intentions

So I'm sorry that my clumsy words

and my even clumsier actions hurt you

I guess now you can sing all those songs about me

all those songs of cruel women

I used to love

until I became one

In my eyes

I'm too wild

a creature to be roped to one lover

to be constrained

I shoot my ancient arrows far in new direction

travelling through air

gaining distance every moment

I push people away because I know

I am most free on my own

burn

I have too much love

in here

caged, compressed in red muscle

Lord, I'm going to

burn

from this warmth

if I can't

share it soon

picket fences

I'm relieved

without you by my side

without your constant cough

without your tormented smile

I see too much of myself in your eyes

deep tree brown

dark

my reflections there inside

I'm relieved to have my freedom back

I can do whatever

(whomever)

I please

Days turn to months

yellow daisies turn to dandelions

those wispy seeds

floating through azure air

after basking in the morning light

after dancing in honeymoon skies

they float to the ground and

like that

tomorrows daisies are alive

I'm relieved, you see

but when your arms

guide their way around mine

that safety is unparalleled

There is no bad in this world

this world of duality

this world I was brought into with hatred

my awareness shaped by fear

there could never be evil in this world

Not with you here

You have a way

of making me melt

making me strip my layers

of insecurity

anxiety

paranoia

it melts away

in your arms

I really hate to admit this part

but as soon as I see

those curly locks

I think of white picket fences

of curly haired children

a pink painted house

with healthy hydrangeas

with marri trees

higher than the tallest of skies

I see those children running

barefoot

amongst the grassy fields

with their arms outstretched

with love in their hearts

belonging to the world

into which I brought them

I can't even remember how long it's been now

but I agreed to see you

my lust for nature

perhaps for experience

(perhaps for you)

brought me here

to this place

this place where there can only be love

Here with you and I

I can be myself

truly childlike

running through these fields

following visions I had of younger souls

You tell me I look brighter

I know this to be true

because I feel myself

so light

burning fiercely

in love for the first time in a while

I could die here

with you

an old woman

outside this blue weatherboard house

underneath the same coloured skies

where spirits meet the clouds

the earth talks through you

I'm wrapped in my crochet blanket

pink and brown circles of wool

I could die here

with you

With my dried up paint brushes

and half-finished canvases

with my wrinkled eyes

and my crooked smile

with my dirtied feet

and bruised legs

with my tired body

and full heart

with tears of wonder in my eyes

I could die

for I have no fear

Not with you here

"It will be quiet soon, don't worry"

his lips parted

I felt like a lamb

young and folly

prancing in those yellow daisy fields`

ready for slaughter

at the hands of love

God, I felt so young

dying in your arms

GAIA

something to look forward to

I will be an old woman

seeing eucalypts

through my jaded eyes

knitting on my porch

on a cane wicker chair

my panting kelpie by my side

I'll have wrinkled hands

silver gemstone rings

cradling a cup of tea

I'll drink it black

swishing it past where my

crooked teeth used to be

Lines engraved by the edges of my lips

deepened through years

decades of living

through love without fear

Strands of hair

now white and wispy

drift amongst the breeze

in blue airplane skies

my gentle voice

following the spirits

lullabies with ease

I'll listen to the mudlarks

the lorikeets and the trees

I'll listen to soft whispers

of the butterflies and the bees

I would be wise and

I would be weathered

I would be blissfully alone

finally

I would have found my freedom

in this sanctuary I call

Home

heart

Under bridges of bone

a fiery core

oozes lava onto volcanic soil

pulsing radiance

destructive yet fertile

rich red ribs

I form mountainous landscapes

with the passionate

magma in my chest

and the ocean that

lapps at my minds shores

bees

With a buzz

they're off!

Evaporated into the azure skies

like the water that

weighed down their wings before

Like time or fate

my trembling hands reached into

the chlorine poison to greet them

fuzzy and yellow

friendly and helpful

they say drowning is the most peaceful

way to go

Though it hurts me to see them

making ripples of panic in the pool

which will surely sink them

as they attempt to quench their thirst

on a thirty degree day

working hard like a builder in the sun

Building the foundations

of life itself   .

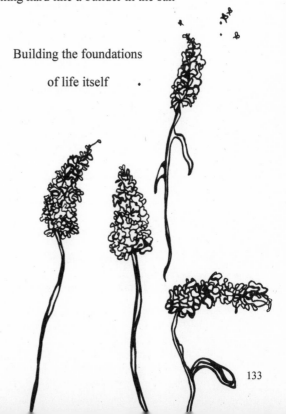

worship

I want prickles to pierce my soles

through a paddock of dried grass

soil between the skin of my toes and nails

God, I want to swim naked in a sea

of salty currents

swirling crystals

galaxies in sunbeams

which pierce the surface

reaching my seaweed hair in golden rays

I want to sit beneath a hollow tree

with moss and vine

a skyscraper in a city of green

with antennae residents

hardworking towns in exoskeleton

business wear

I belong out here

mountains grow taller than

concrete structures

and kiss the forming clouds farewell

welcoming in their place

the rising sun

rivers flow stronger than all that stands in their path

where stars burn brighter

than lights ever could

and the moon shines

beyond your wildest imaginings

leaves whisper tales of

a hundred years seen before you

and the breeze sings songs

that paint stories

if you open your ears

Where death is merely the beginning of life

and dreams form reality

I want the wind on my breast, the sand on my legs, the sea in my ears, salt encrusted on the ends of my eyelashes, the sun kissing my skin golden brown, the flowers delighting my nose, the trees pressed against my gentle grasp, the rain in my hair, waterfalls in my mouth, crisp water engulfing my chest, the cliffs beneath my toes, the grass brushing my ankles, the clear sky in my eyes, fresh fruit on my tongue, dirt under my nails, insect bites along the length of my thigh, to breathe heavy exhilarating euphoric gasps of fresh crisp breeze, to feel warm light on my back.

I want

to worship this planet

the way she deserves

I want

to feel one and liberated

with the earth that gave me the greatest gift of all

life

meteor

I am not a shooting star

don't make wishes on me

I am more a meteor

crashing towards earth

one day I'll land

one day I'll feel grounded

one day my atoms

will belong

in this atmosphere

unconscious

I wish I could make the unconscious see

the goodness swimming beneath the surface

of a greed driven humanity

fawn

Clovers to carry

the soft sleeping belly

of a wounded child

I am cradled

harmonious in earthly arms

like fawn beneath fox

fatal

these sores fade to infinite

for she collects death

to gain

tears to sublime rain

watering her roots

who once nourished me

feed from my flesh

so I'm reborn again

a quiet letter to me

I hope I never lose sight of myself

never losing my gratitude

remaining eternally humble

for we are born equals

and to dirt

we shall return

equal

fertiliser for mother earth's beauties

why should I believe my life

my soul

my body

be more valuable

than anyone else

rabbits

A creeping child

a predator

I hid beneath the bush

tracking my brother and father

Beady innocent eyes

peeking through dried copse

at last a creature emerges

leaping in great hops

I adored following gentle beasts

running fast as I could

my childish feet with each passing beat

running towards the woods

She sat, alert, great ears perked high

though I hadn't drawn a breath

in the frightened air

she turned to glare

then ran from her sure death

Stomping leaden footfalls

is what she heard before

my human ears failed

as it unfolded

kneeling beside a tuft of grass

his hands reached the floor

there I bore horrifying witness

to great metal jaws

of strength and steel

entrapping her paws

Sharpened metal teeth

cut through her soft bones

like a bread knife with your meal

her body twitching as she groaned

Not with her feeble voice

too weak to cry out in vain

a shift in the childlike air

the earth and I both felt her pain

Her family had abandoned her

thudded their huge feet

with fear

sorrow

and heavy hearts

they made their prompt retreat

It was my father who held her by the legs

soon my brothers turn

to twist her neck

to snap her bones

he enjoyed it

I discerned

What I find most easy to recall

that awful crack ringing in my ears

her furry body limp that summer evening

and my eyes brimming with tears

I screamed with such gravity

I'd never used or raised

dad's eyes looked so foreign

dangerous

as they met my gaze

"They're pests, Freya

vermin

they need to be exterminated"

"Humans" I replied

with a heavy heart

"are the pests that need to be terminated"

taste the love

The Life

The Death

The Afterlife

Three Black Ravens whom I see

(everywhere)

only two can be seen here

flying through dismal skies

over these paddocks

where the air is metallic

stench of fear

screams echo over the valleys

Taste the love

Men in white coats soon

to be painted red

men with whips

whooping like a wild beast

(he's enjoying this)

Sticking sticks on their backsides

prodding them down the ramps of death

this crow perched

waiting

Taste the love

He looked into my eyes with such depth

one blue eye, one brown

looking

searching

yearning

for compassion he'd never seen

make home in my species

I felt helplessness

I felt him saying "save me"

as the wheels screeched

through the gates of hell

Taste the love

In my mind I visualised

his blue eyes bloodshot

with fear

drenched with shit

suffocating

slowly twitching

lungs burning black

losing consciousness

in a dark cage of carbon dioxide

Taste the love

willow

I fly with my

great eyed wings

through vents of warm air

Whispers from leaves

gliding effortlessly

my outstretched arms

whipped by the wind

this

I think

is freedom

This

I think

is home

For I was born a monarch spirit

on a strange trip through cosmic carnations

of earth children

beady-eyed and greedy

ungrateful and unsatisfied

I

humbled and free

not anchored to fear

let

myself

breathe

and

leave

As I emerge through the chrysalis

of human form

through ego identity

On six wispy legs

I found the place

within my crimson heart

in crystalline eyes

where my soul lies

stellium

I feel the thrills of adolescence

in my mind

I never grew

from the trials of time

Although I feel

the weight of womanhood on my chest

the weight of wisdom on my shoulders

I float a feather in the winds

light as the air she glides with truth

I live my days in imagination

under Apollo's rule

in the kingdom of youth

dryandra

Dryandra moth on harvest moon

sticky December night

beats his dampened tawny wings

to make his humble flight

O' the moth seldom ceases

his lonesome flight

save for when he sources

warm golden light

and what he uncovered

on my breast that day

was a raging wildfire

of love and grace

I hope perhaps I

may be for you

what this spirit sign

has taught me to do

A little moth

to guide your way

towards light

through darkness and decay

A little moth to take your hand

to find the light within you

and show you where to land

summer rain i

Droplets on the feathered outlines

of eucalyptus leaf

dusty blue and green

like smoke settled

on the gum trees

after years of

ceremonial harvest

Falling to leaf litter

Puddles and pools

for centipedes

as centimetres grow

so too does the smell

wet limestone

hurried ants

The air is quiet

thick with liquid

to quench the thirst of a

whole hungry hoard

of trees and wallabies

You can feel the red dirt sing

"Hallelujah!"

as her pores are kissed

by gentle summer mist

summer rain ii

In the humid summer air, the warm breeze

the smokey haze, the ever-patient trees

waiting for Gaia to water their roots

Her rain fell gently that night

it rattled

a motorbike on the tin roof

we heard crickets clapping their legs

singing

in joyous harmony

Those droplets of water met my parched skin

melted into my pores

dancing with the dirt

my skin collected that day

washed away

with it

my agony

youniverse

It is difficult to remain small

when you feel

an entire universe forming

from branches in your heart

rainbow serpent

Feebly following the flock

a sheep

held on the leash by hand of greed

take the reigns

be the serpent who forms valleys

in the desert

who brings water

to the mountains

who unearths the truth with his

scaly skin

be the venom

that heals all who drink

from dripping fangs

Next time you believe

that you are only one person

you make no real difference

understand that

if you keep those doe eyes closed

you will never experience your divinity

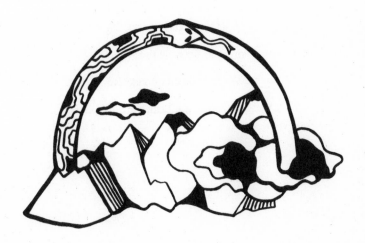

oceans iii

Clouds streamed

across gradient sky

two golden arrows

pointed towards the line

under which the sun sleeps

Too wild to be woman

too domesticated to be wolf

I run

my roar fierce in the wind

bare feet brushing concrete

burning hot my leathery soles

waves hitting with every thud

heavy oceans in my body

my heart the moon

controlling the tides

I crash

I erode

Running on hot sand

the skeletons of many before me

the most beautiful graveyard

clings to my living skin

like magnets to my bony frame

I dive

a heron

into crystal waters

everything

The universe whispered to my ears

through gentle breeze

"Everything you need is within you

Everything you desire is within your reach

Everything you fear forms in your mind

Everything you love is a reflection of yourself"

"You and I are more alike than you believe

You are the universe experiencing itself

dancing though life"

you

We are the creators of our own reality

through pain we struggle

We spiral outwards, damaging others with our collateral path

of crude rudeness and sheer ignorance of other's emotions

we're clumsy because subconsciously we believe it to be so

that we are hurting more than most

Our pain body awakens and longs to drag others down to join

him

Everyone's pain is relative to their own experience

to each

their pain may seem excruciating and just as much as

the other

It is all about

COMPASSION

EMPATHY

But here is the real trick

No matter what situation you find yourself in
only you control how you react

You choose to feel your sadness
you choose to dwell in pain
you choose not to move a finger

Sometimes healing means moving

MOUNTAINS

With your bare hands
ultimately the only person who can transform your
perspective
attitude
outlook

is you

So forget feeling claustrophobic

with the weight of the world pushing against your frail body

and arthritic bones

you hold the power of the universe inside of yourself

Reach in

Burn your hands in the

golden light

Radiate outwards

so others may shine in your rays

You are your own saviour

You are your own healer

You are your own god

You are your only reality

So make it count today

and every day

chrysalis

Great and green she towered

over my humble body

vines hanging to the soles of my feet

sun creeping through breaks

in the sweet-smelling leaves

perched upon them

a bundle of brown seedy shells

translucent and glowing

buzzing with ethereal life

I see reflections

my fleshy face and that

great mop of salty hair

I carry on my shoulders

in my eyes

a spark

their mother

reborn in the summer

Beautiful and orange

shifting with each soft wisp of wind

making invisible waves

ripples in the humid air

psychedelic patterns

of perfumed cosmos

catching my kaleidoscope eyes

I walked the streets

ecstatic overjoyed

drugged and drunk by spring pollen

nature's love potion

My fear clouded

with hazel love vast and open

as those welcoming wings

seemed to disappear in the night

their numbers falling rapidly

with each summers breath

I felt myself going with them

through that colourful void

unto the world of eternal spirit

the afterlife

I was pulled

strand by strand in the cyclone

an anchor tethered to my weary heart

My physical self remained unscathed

I prepared for

and experienced

death

metamorphosis

mental disorientation

illness of the mind

I awoke

tasting nectar of the gods

sangria delighting my tastebuds

the finest of wines

laced with zeal

lust

ecstasy

no longer the monarch

I was reborn

with fresh eyes and an old soul

I was reborn

with love in my eyes

and flowers in my hair

THANK YOU

So I say thank you, reader.

Thank you for your patience in reading this part of me. Thank you for listening to my voice after I spent the majority of my life as mute. With coals in my throat I never allowed my heart to be heard.

This project, this part of my life is so precious to me.

By allowing my words, my experiences, my pain, love and fear to be on these pages, my heart bleeds ink. I am finally able to shamelessly share my experiences. Finally am I able to trust in myself, trust in the world.

So thank you.

From the deepest parts of the caverns of my heart

I thank you.

You are loved,

You are.

a space for thoughts and drawing...